This page is intentionally left blank.

This page is intentionally left blank.

Social Sales.
The Book.

This page is intentionally left blank.

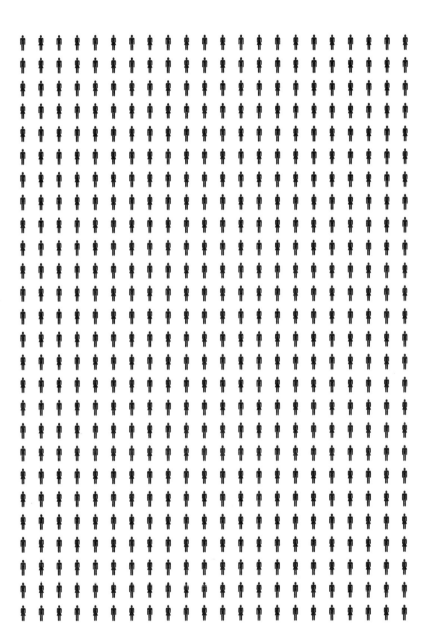

Production & Publishing:
Books on Demand GmbH,
Norderstedt, Germany.

ISBN 9783842382435

Social Sales.
The Book.

Shake up your B2B sales by leveraging the power of
collaboration, social networks and CRM.

«If I had more time, I would write you a shorter letter.»
Johann Wolfgang von Goethe, 1767

Kiss.

With the rise of the Internet, the way we manage and consume information has dramatically changed. In this book, we are reflecting this by keeping it short and simple. Some of the underlying concepts we are introducing do fill entire bookshelves. But the idea of this book is to compress the key messages in a few simple sentences and no more than 5 bullet points.

On top, we do explain and underline complex models by using side notes, comments and quotes that will be regularly updated.

As a result, you are holding an interactive compendium in your hands, the encyclopedia of Social Sales.

Win. Grow. Social Sales.

No-one likes to loose. But we all do. And there are good excuses like price, features and our administrative workload. We also know that providing a discount is not selling. But yes, we all do. And we all remember situations finding ourselves talking to the wrong audience...

With Social Sales, we can change the rules by focusing on what is really important: The people and social relationships behind the deal.

This book is designed for the visionaries and game changers applying «Social Sales» to increase B2B sales effectiveness.

It is targeted to sales, account, marketing and business managers who want to invest in their social capital in order to succeed in relationship-driven sales environments.

The objective is to help sales teams to win strategic opportunities and grow their target accounts.

Storyline

The content of this book is structured into 5 distinctive chapters. Since most topics are presented in a closed way, you can read it from right to left or back to front depending on your interest. To breathe the full story we recommend you to start with the environmental background presented in the first chapters.

I. People Business
Sales is about people. Period?

II. Buyside
No selling without buying. The customer perspective.

III. Salesside
B2B sales can be very challenging. In this chapter, we will summarize some of the most popular concepts, processes and methodologies for you.

IV. Social Business
The building blocks of social businesses: Thought leadership on social media, social networks and collaboration.

V. Social Sales
How does a SocialSalesMap look like? What is a SocialSalesIndex? And how can a SocialSalesMatrix help you in defining the most effective action plan?

Bonus Material: We are working on it.

Sales is about people. Period?

The world of sales is changing dramatically. Buyer networks. Social Business. Collaborative CRM. What strategic options do we have to differentiate in the marketplace and grow our sales?

I. People Business

«Executives need to push their organizations toward becoming fully networked enterprises.»

«A new class of company is emerging—one that uses collaborative Web 2.0 technologies intensively to connect the internal efforts of employees and to extend the organization's reach to customers, partners, and suppliers. We call this new kind of company the networked enterprise. Results from our analysis of proprietary survey data show that the Web 2.0 use of these companies is significantly improving their reported performance. In fact, our data show that fully networked enterprises are not only more likely to be market leaders or to be gaining market share but also use management practices that lead to margins higher than those of companies using the Web in more limited ways.»

McKinsey & Company,
"The rise of the networked enterprise: Web 2.0 finds its payday.",
April 2011.

Managing Complexity

The world of sales is changing dramatically. Driven by internationalization and latest information technologies, B2B sales has become more complex than ever before.

1. Buyer Networks
Value chains are being transformed into networks. Hierarchies have turned into collaborative communities and virtual teamwork further accelerates distributed decision-making. As a result, buyer decision models are being fundamentally transformed.

2. Social Business
On top, social media, networks and business software are completely changing the way we communicate and engage with people, internally as well as externally. Gathering information about sellers and buyers in real-time has never been easier providing threats and opportunities at the same time.

The future success of sales organizations depends on how well they are able to adapt to the above changes in the marketplace. It also means that selling roles will be changing.

Are you ready?

«It is taught in kindergarten that sharing is a nice thing to do. The same rule applies in business, at least when it comes to the type of CRM known as collaborative CRM.»

«Collaborative CRM aims to get various departments within a business, such as sales, technical support and marketing, to share the useful information that they collect from interactions with customers. Feedback from a tech-support center, for example, could be used to inform marketing staffers about specific services and features requested by customers. Collaborative CRM's ultimate goal is to use information collected from all departments to improve the quality of customer service, and, as a result, increase customer satisfaction and loyalty.»

InsideCRM
"Get it together with collaborative CRM",
November 2007.

The evolution of CRM.

In the past, customer relationship management (CRM) was mainly used to streamline processes and running detailed analysis and reports. By adding collaborative aspects, CRM gets a whole new dimension.

1. Transactional
Running marketing and sales operations efficiently requires a high level of process optimization. This is especially true for service organizations or in classical product sales using push technologies.

2. Analytical
Analyzing customers, regions and SKU's left and right is the fundament of data-driven, intelligent sales. Specific reports can be used to segment markets, identify target accounts and maximize conversion rates.

3. Collaborative
Working together on projects and opportunities leveraging the power of social technologies, can also help to achieve targets, not just to report on them.

Collaboration is not necessarily new. Nor is CRM. But making CRM collaborative is a great opportunity to maximize the outcome of sales investments. At the end, it is about effectiveness, not just efficiency.

«If you don't have a competitive advantage,
don't compete.»
Jack Welch, Former CEO, General Electric

Competitive Differentiation

There is three ways for companies to create competitive advantages.

1. Product Leadership
It means delivering superior products, solutions and services by investing into innovation, design & technology. Apple and Tetra Pak are good examples.

2. Operational Excellence
It is about optimizing processes to achieve advantages in terms of time, cost and quality. Dell aims to lead the PC business regarding process efficiency. General Electric (GE) has invested heavily into six sigma to become quality leader.

3. Customer Intimacy
Investing into your social capital to build intimate customer relationships is the most rewarding strategy in the majority of project and solution businesses. By better understanding the needs and wants of your customers, you will enjoy a higher win rate, achieve a price premium and more repeat business. IBM and McKinsey are good benchmarks in this category.

Social Sales is a way of applying operational excellence in selling to achieve customer intimacy.

What competitive strategy do you have?

«People don't care how much you know, until they know how much you care.»

Theodore Roosevelt, 26th President of the United States

Sales is about people.

In theory, business decisions are made in a very analytical, un-emotional way. This might be true in most cases, but parts of the analytics are soft decision-criteria that can make a real difference.

1. Trust
Customers want to minimize risk. Successful sales is about being trusted and viewed as a respectable as well as credible partner.

2. Relationship
People buy from people they like. Having a positive relationship means access to the right information and having the opportunity to interact. Relationship matters.

3. Individual Needs
Understanding the career ambitions, agenda and personal interests of people is equally important then the business case itself. The more you can step up and take responsibility for the individual needs and wants, the higher the value you create, the higher the premium you get.

It doesn't matter whether you are selling a product frame agreement, a service project or a technical solution. The best business proposal is useless if you cannot identify, engage and manage the right people effectively.

«What if you added more reps?»

What if you increased investments in lead generation to create more opportunities? What if you reduced the no decision rate by a few percentage points/or increased you win rates against competitors? How about figuring out how to remove some of the admin burden from your sales people so they have more time to actually sell?

CSO Insights,
"Revenue 2012: Making it Happen Versus Hoping it Happens",
January 2012.

Growth Options

Do you plan to increase sales this year? Let's assume for a second that demand, offering and competition will be stable, what options do you have to grow your sales?

1. Increase Salesforce
Depending on your market coverage, hiring new sales employees should give you the capacity to acquire additional business, directly or indirectly. The challenge is to train and coach them effectively, keeping lead times in mind. This is even more true for entering new markets.

2. Increase Sales Efficiency
In B2B, salespeople often spend some 30% of their time on administrative tasks. Reducing the admin effort and/or offloading internal activities to sales assistants or operation centers, will free time for selling. You will also see positive impact on the average cost of sales (COS).

3. Increase Sales Effectiveness
Keep the team, but increase the outcome (win rate). Social Sales aims to help you achieve more with the same resources by extending and capitalizing on your social relationships.

Where do you see the highest impact? What's the best mix for your business?

No selling without buying.

Before jumping into the sales discussions, let's look on it from the customer perspective first. How are complex buying decisions being made? How does a typical buying cycle look like? Which roles are involved? What impact does the personality have on individual decision-making? And how are suppliers being managed most effectively?

II. Buyside

«The shift from hierarchical leadership to tribal leadership makes it clear that social architectures don't need control; they need trust.»

«As we are witnessing the end of the Industrial Revolution, we discover that leadership and workplace dynamics are no longer hierarchical. That game is over. We need to take into account the fact that the internet is fundamentally changing the DNA of workplace dynamics.»

Luc Galoppin,
"Social Architecture, a Manifesto"
January 2011.

Buying Decision Model

In the past, decisions have been made in silos and by Patriarchs. Today, extensive collaboration across complex buyer networks is reality. We can differentiate the following buying decision models:

1. Hierarchical
Classical top-down approach. Decisions are being prepared by the Indians and decided by the chiefs.

2. Decentralized
Local organizations are entitled to decide based on their individual needs.

3. Collaborative
Diverse, multidisciplinary and open teams are working together to find the best solution.

4. Buyer Networks
External influencers like partners, suppliers, experts and institutions are actively integrated into the decision process.

There is a clear downshift, with dramatic impact on any sales organization. We have to learn how to effectively manage and succeed as part of complex value networks.

The Buying Cycle

Today's buying journey consists of a mix of interactions across different channels and networks. However, the traditional buying cycle still applies behind the scenes.

1. Awareness
An initial stimulus let the discussion start. This could be an internal problem escalation, a marketing interaction or just a coincidental meeting.

2. Consideration
Depending on the potential, the customer forms a first buying intention and actively gathers information to satisfy its needs. Typically, at this point, you will have the first sales meeting.

3. Preference
A detailed analysis will let the customer narrow down different alternatives. Often, a structured RFQ process is being used. At the end, there should be a preliminary decision.

4. Action
So if you don't mess up in final negotiations or run into unacceptable contractual terms, the purchase is being formalized.

5. Loyalty
There's a great opportunity to intensify the relationship during delivery and if maintained well, trigger re-purchases, up- and cross-sell business.

ZMOT

What has really changed is that the customer now has the opportunity to do intensive research by herself using search engines and social media, without and before talking to a supplier. That is, what Google calls the "Zero Moment of Truth" (ZMOT).

1. Stimulus
The awareness phase.

2. ZMOT
The customer researches potential solutions, compares products and prices, follows discussions and reads reviews. Online.

3. Shelf
The first touchpoint with the potential product, service or solution. In the B2B world, this might be your sales presentation.

4. Experience
The second, "real" point of truth. Does the solution keep its promises when using?

As a result, you will meet a better informed customer who often already has a preference in mind before talking to you. So the best way is to be the stimulus yourself to trigger the direction the customer takes. And to work with existing customers to provide positive online reviews and case studies to positively influence the ZMOT.

Buying Criteria.

Interestingly, buying criteria are traditionally changing along the buying journey.

1. Need
Identifying a business issue and analyzing its root cause triggers the start of a new buying process. The need is the most important subject of the discussion.

2. Solution
Second, we can look into alternative solutions addressing it. What are the pros and cons?

3. Cost
If the solution and its related value are understood, the buyer intends to minimize costs in order to improve the ROI. Often, the purchase department comes into play.

4. Risk
At the end of the buying cycle, risk is the dominant factor. So if the buyer starts to ask the "risk" questions, you are coming to an end. The business case is being completed.

How are group decisions being made?

According to studies of behavioral science, the interaction of groups in decision-making can be structured into different phases.

1. Orientation
This is the warm-up phase, where people start to meet and interact with each other.

2. Conflict
Once the group is being formed, there's a healthy phase of arguing and discussing, not just on facts, but also on positions.

3. Emergence
Different views and opinions are consolidated into a common picture.

4. Reinforcement
Once the decision is being made, members will try to defend it, internally as well as externally.

Most probably you will recognize above behaviors in most buying decisions of your customers. But let's also keep in mind that decisions are rarely being made in isolated groups, but in complex networks. For the good and the bad.

Roles

Today, roles are more important than functions. It's the hat(s) that someone has in a project, not the imprint on her business card, which makes the difference.

1. Budget Owner
The ones sitting on the money to fund the exercise. In enterprises, budget owners might be very different from the ones receiving the value.

2. Contract Signatory
Usually, two persons with power of procuration will put their signature under the final contract.

3. Opportunity Owner
Who is having the lead on solving the problem on customer side? Who is driving the deal from the partner and from our side?

4. Proposal Lead
The person running the RFP process. In our team, the member responsible for preparing the bid.

5. Subject Matter Expert
Specialists or trusted advisors that do the technical or functional assessment or build the vision.

6. Ultimate Authority
Who is doing the final, final go/no go decision?

Psychology - The People Side of Business

At the end of the day, we are selling to people, not companies.

According to psychology, the personality of every person can be classified into a mixture of 3 main structures.

1. Red
This is the emotional, dominant, dynamic side of life. Red personalities love to win and would like you to go the extra mile.

2. Green
Green characters are very communicative, nice and relaxed persons. They value harmony and personal relationships.

3. Blue
Blue signals fact-based, analytical and serious behavior. Blue characters need to be convinced with arguments and strong cases.

Understanding the characteristics, needs and interests of people is the first step of finding the right sales approach to turn challengers into champions.

Cognitive Styles

Another way, to look at it, is the Myers-Briggs Type Indicator (MBTI). It captures a person's behavior across four polarizing dimensions.

1. Extroversion (E) vs. Introversion (I)
This parameter describes the general attitude of a person, which can be used to engage with her.

2. Sensing (S) vs. Intuition (N)
This pair is capturing the irrational, perceiving function. This attitude is mainly used while gathering information.

3. Thinking (T) vs. Feeling (F)
This behavior is called the rational or judging function. It is especially important in decision making. A thinker will seek for a reasonable, process-oriented and analytical approach. Instead, a feeler will try to balance the interests, seek consensus and trust her instinct.

4. Judgment (J) vs. Perception (P)
The lifestyle set analyzes, whether the perceiving or judging functions are dominating. Is the person rather strong in preparing the story or in closing the discussions?

It can also be applied to explain cross-cultural differences in decision-making.

Supplier Relationship Management (SRM)

The idea of effective supplier relationship management (SRM) is segmenting the entire portfolio into manageble groups depending on factors like volume, value and variability. By using different collaboration models within each segment, the buyer can make best use of their resources as well as the supplier capabilities.

A Strategic
You are trusted and respected to contribute to the long-term business objectives of the buyer. You are expected to create value by effective collaboration beyond delivery.

B Tactical
You might still sell significant volumes with certain interdependencies, however your contribution is limited to satisfy a specific demand. There is little influence on the specification or strategic direction of the customer.

C Transactional
You are seen as non-critical by the buyer. Perceived differentiation and switching costs are low.

The Art and Science of Selling

B2B sales can be very challenging. It requires broad knowledge, practical experience and especially senior management skills. In this chapter, we will summarize some of the most popular concepts, processes and methodologies for you. The topics range from qualifying opportunities, increasing forecast accuracy, getting the most out of a sales meeting up to managing risks and lifetime value. Depending on your specific sales environment, not all of it will apply to you, but it's good to keep the concepts in mind to stay on top of your sales opportunities at any point in time.

III. Salesside

Sales Strategies

There are 2 fundamental sales strategies. Farmers will earn a price premium, while hunters will keep your cost-of-sales low.

1. Farming
Developing a target account strategically can be a challenging and time-consuming task. The fruits are sustainable relationships and strategic insights. If you believe, that long-term partnerships are crucial to your business, seed.

2. Hunting
Hunters are focusing on low-hanging fruits instead. The goal is not to become a trusted advisor, but to win that particular opportunity and then move on to the next. It can be most effective to work with B and C accounts or markets.

Depending how relationship-intensive your business or industry is, you will meet more farmers or hunters. But most often, you will see a mix of both working in parallel.

Sales Stages

Without process, you simply can't manage your sales activities strategically. Following a structured process, will enable effective planning, collaboration and especially resource allocation.

1. Discovery
A potential sales opportunity is being identified.

2. Qualification
Does the opportunity meet our bid criteria?

3. Pre-Proposal
Analyzing key needs by active listening. Here, you can take the most influence shaping the customer needs and wants.

4. Proposal
In close collaboration with the customer and partners, a formal offer is being provided.

5. Negotiation
Final terms and conditions are being agreed upon.

6. Award
The contract is being signed. Start of delivery.

In general, the earlier the interaction with the customer and partners, the better, so you cannot just maximize your influence but also come to an early go/no go decision.

«As a rule of thumb,
orders always take 2 times longer and are 1/2 the volume.»
Felix Mayer, CEO, Sensirion AG.

Forecasting

Accurate forecasting is not rocket science, if you have a good pipeline management in place.

1. Opportunity Probability
What is the likelihood of the opportunity to be awarded? Are the qualification criteria fulfilled? Will there be any organizational changes? Is the business climate stable?

2. Chance to Win
Assuming the project will be awarded, what are our chances to win compared to the competition? How many vendors are involved at the different buying stages? Do we have good or superior relationships and/or value propositions?

3. Weighted Forecast
An opportunity of 1mio with a probability of 80% and a 50% chance of winning makes up 400,000 in the books. Simple, but effective.

4. Weighted Value
On top you might want to consider the strategic value of entering new markets, cracking a reference account or winning a pilot project. Whatever factor you apply, make sure it is also reflected in the compensation plan, so the sales team matches their level of effort.

The more you automate the process, the more time for selling. Tying it strictly to the sales stages and their qualification criteria will leave no room for interpretation.

BANT

Asking the BANT questions at an early stage ensures to focus our limited resources on the "real" opportunities.

1. Budget
Is the potential funding of the deal secured? Does the sponsor have enough cash to pay for the total expenses?

2. Authority
Do we have access to the "real" decision-makers? Can we leverage any direct or indirect relationships to the person in charge?

3. Need
Does the customer have a latent or explicit need? Is there a problem to be solved?

4. Timeline
Is there a clear timeframe to resolve the problem? Do you feel a certain sense of urgency? Has the customer set any milestones for decision-making?

Yes, we have a qualified opportunity. So there is real demand. But what is our chance of winning?

AIDA

Classical sales pitches follow the AIDA principle.

1. Attention

Entry question, joke or story. "Did you know that SuperCompany doubled their win rate by engaging in Social Sales?"

2. Interest

Facts. Facts. Facts. What's the problem? What's the solution? What are the key features and benefits?

3. Desire

Explain the value proposition. Potential impact. Reason-to-buy. Proof-Points. Why now?

4. Action

Get a specific deliverable or commitment from the customer side. Next steps?

While a lot has changed since the introduction of solution selling concepts, there still might be moments within the sales process where it is highly effective to follow the AIDA principle.

Just think of your next proposal presentation.

Solution Selling

Solution selling is complex in practice, but simple in theory.

1. Identify Problem
Are there any pain points the customer experiences? Can we pinpoint the root cause? And what's the impact for her business?

2. Need
A problem turns into a need if the customer is prepared to fix it.

3. Solution
There are many ways of satisfying a specific need. The challenge is to help the buyer build a vision for a solution, which outbeats alternatives.

4. Value
The best solution will remain on shelve, unless we can help the buyer to justify the costs and risks associated. If we have a superior value proposition, it's time to put it on the table now.

Managing Risks

Life is about risks, especially sales life. At the end of the buying cycle, risk becomes the most important decision criteria for the buyer, so we have the chance to positively influence the decision.

In quantitative risk analysis, the following parameters are being used to prioritize and decide whether to enter a specific risk or mitigate.

1. Probability
What's the likelihood of a specific event to occur?

2. Impact
In case the event happens, what is the magnitude of the potential loss?

3. Effort
What's the cost of mitigating the risk? In case of uncertainty due to lack of information, it can be rather low. But sometimes a complex proof-of-concept or contingency plan might be needed to convince the customer.

At the end, probability times impact minus effort gives the customer an idea whether a possible mitigation would see a positive ROI or not.

Sales KPI

What you can't measure, you can't manage. Using the most appropriate sales KPI for your business will help you to take your sales to the next level.

1. Response Rate
For any sales and marketing campaign, how many contacts from the target community make use of the call-to-action, e.g. visiting the landing page, ordering a sample or requesting a service?

2. Conversion Rate
It tells us how much effort it takes to transfer a visitor, contact or lead into a qualified opportunity.

3. Bid Rate
From all the requests we receive, in what percentage of potential sales volume have we made an offer?

4. Hit Rate
From all offers made, what volume percentage have we won? Since it also includes cancelled opportunities, it tells us whether we have put the efforts on the right place.

5. Win Rate
Measured against the volume of awarded opportunities, what percentage did we finally win against competition?

Customer Satisfaction

In most businesses, the typical sales effort for keeping existing customers is just 10-20% of winning new ones. Increasing customer satisfaction and stimulating cross- and upselling should be a priority for every sales team.

1. Repurchase Rate
The repurchase rate is a good indicator for how satisfied new customers are and whether your products, solutions and services have met their expectations.

2. Retention Rate
Managed well, the renewal of service contracts or frame agreements is a great opportunity to ensure a constant revenue stream from existing customers.

3. Net Promoter Score (NPS)
With NPS, you can measure and compare what percentage of customers will be very likely to recommend your product, service or solution to a friend or colleague (promoters) versus the unlikely ones (detractors). There is a direct correlation between NPS and company growth.

4. Lifetime Value
What's the average contribution a new customer of a specific type brings throughout the product/solution lifecycle? In other words: What's the cross- and upsell potential for new customers? For many investment goods like machinery or software, the service business exceeds the new business by factor 2 or more. This figure tells you how aggressive you can be in acquiring new customers.

Top5 Sales Questions

Questions are the answers. Here are the top 5 qualification questions.

1. Why?
Is there a specific customer need?

2. What?
Do we have a competitive solution to address the problem?

3. Who?
Do we know the key players in the buyer network?

4. How?
Do we have a good sales strategy and action plan to win?

5. When?
Is the timing right? When will the existing contract expire or when does the existing equipment need to be replaced?

III. Salesside.

This page is intentionally left blank.

The building blocks of social businesses.

The social media revolution is still very young but has fundamentally changed the way we communicate and exchange information, for individuals and businesses alike. We are still in the process of learning how to utilize social communities and networks most effectively. However, it is a pleasure to present some of the thought leadership on social media, social networks and collaboration in the following. Today, we cannot imagine a company without email or Internet presence. In the future, there will be no company without social media engagement and social collaboration, not just related to marketing and sales.

IV. Social Business

«As the world becomes more instrumented,
interconnected and intelligent and the population
continues to embrace social computing, today's enterprises
face the dawn of a new era –
the era of the Social Business.»

«Just as the Internet changed the marketplace forever, the integration of social computing into enterprise design represents another enormous shift in the landscape. Organizations that successfully transform into a Social Business can potentially reap great benefits – among them the ability to deepen customer relationships, drive operational efficiencies and optimize the workforce.»

IBM Corporation,
"The Social Business - Advent of a new age",
February 2011.

Social Media Opportunities

Whether in sales, marketing or service, providing a great customer experience also means making effective use of social networks and media.

1. Listen
The first step of every social media engagement is to understand the different channels, conversations and opportunities by effective Social Media Monitoring (SMM) and Analysis.

2. Engage
Providing interactive support is a great way to collaborate with existing and potential customers alike. Technical communities can build the first level of trust required for future touchpoints.

3. Promote
Social media marketing is the art of using social media channels to increase marketing reach and awareness.

4. Learn
Finally, social media can be used to co-innovate with customers and partners by crowdsourcing ideas and continuously gathering market feedback.

POEM

The Paid, Owned, Earned Media (POEM) framework is a powerful tool to understand the new media environment.

1. Owned
The good thing with owned content is that you have full control of it, might it be your websites, online stores, apps, newsletters or social network profiles. Here, you can maintain relationships and stimulate cross- and upselling.

2. Paid
Banner ads or paid search engine marketing can be a great source to increase awareness and generate traffic. While response rates are declining, it can still provide the required scalability to generate new sales leads.

3. Earned
Obviously, the most credible form of content are external comments, likes, shares, forum entries, blog posts or other forms of word-of-mouth and viral marketing. Establishing a strong community of net promoters is fuel for your sales engine.

While the roles of the different media types are very different for sales and marketing alike, synchronized well, they all play together to help you achieve your overall business goals.

90-9-1 Principle

In Internet communities, forums and social networks we can see a large participation inequality, described by the 90-9-1 rule.

1. Readers
A large majority (90%) of users view content without contributing.

2. Contributors
Some 9% of users edit or modify content.

3. Creators
But only 1% of users create new content.

While this is not necessarily surprising, it is important to keep in mind when using social business software for sales and marketing purposes.

«Social CRM is a business strategy that generates opportunities for sales, marketing and customer service, while also benefiting cloud-based communities.»

«Social CRM applications need to be far more customer-centric than more traditional CRM applications. Without benefits for the customer, communities and social networks die, resulting in no benefits to the organization using the social CRM applications. To be successful with social CRM, organizations need to be much less focused on how an organization can manage the customer, and much more focused on how the customer can manage the relationship.»

Gartner Group,
"Magic Quadrant for Social CRM",
July 2011.

Social CRM

Already today, every salesperson, marketeer and service manager can make effective use of social media. Moving forward, there will be no CRM service without reaching out into social networks anymore.

1. Identify service opportunities
Turning a twitter complaint into a support opportunity.

2. Identify leads
Capture a sales lead from a LinkedIn group or Quora discussion.

3. Identify target audiences
Use social media profiles on Xing or Google Plus to identify potential influencers and decision-makers.

4. Connect
Use existing relationships to reach out and build new relationships in a credible way.

«We believe influence is the ability to drive action.»

«It's great to have lots of connections but what really matters is how people engage with the content you create. We believe it's better to have a small and engaged audience than a large network that doesn't act upon your content.»

Klout,
"Understanding Klout",
2012.

Follow Me.

Ties between people can have many faces, especially in social networks.

1. Subscription
Following someone or something on social media means institutionalizing the interest into a person or group by subscribing to her posts and updates.

2. Connection
Based on mutual agreement, a friendship or connection can be established. In theory, every person is connected with every other person by not more than 5 degrees.

3. Interaction
In social media, an interaction can be commenting, liking, sharing, writing on the wall, mentioning or re-posting. Every interaction is an opportunity to strengthen a relationship.

4. Relationship
A relationship constitutes of the sum of all interactions, online and offline, between two parties. In a network, it represents the flow of information and communication.

In fact, a subscription or connection is a sign of potential influence. But interactions are measurable indicators of relationship intensity.

Social Network Dictionary

1. Edge
Interdependent social relationship (tie, connection, link) between teams and/or persons. Represents the flow of information and communication in a network. Can be directed or undirected.

2. Node
A social entity, either an individual (person, contact) or a team (group, organization).

3. Team
In multi-level networks, persons with common attributes can be grouped together into teams.

4. Bridge
Relationship providing indirect access to other teams and/or persons for introductions or for channeling messages.

5. Gatekeeper
Person providing exclusive access to disconnected teams or persons. Can be used for channeling or need to be bypassed.

6. Hub
Central team or person connected to multiple other teams and/or persons. Good subject for effective targeting.

7. Satellite
Person linked to a central hub.

Social Network Analysis

Social Network Analysis (SNA) studies relationship structures among social entities (teams, persons) in order to assess its social influence and importance.

1. Centrality
Indicates the social influence or importance of a node based on their social connections in a network.

1. Degree Centrality
Measures the number of connections a node owns. It only takes direct relationships into account.

2. Closeness Centrality
Measures the influence based on the shortest paths to any other node. Hubs typically have a high closeness centrality.

3. Betweenness Centrality
Measures the influence based on how often a contact sits on the shortest path connecting other nodes. Gatekeepers typically have a high betweenness centrality.

4. Eigenvector Centrality
Measures the importance of a node by taking into account the strenghts of relationships and influence of directly and indirectly connected nodes. By analyzing sales networks using Eigenvector centrality, the «real» importance of influencers and decision-makers can be assessed.

Law of the Few.

Research suggests, that within a social network, there is a small number of influencers that can make an idea or opinion succeed. This phenomenon is called the law of the few. Malcolm Gladwell differentiates in 3 types of roles that have the particular and rare social gift to create such a social epidemic.

1. Connectors

Connectors are people experts. They own a large social network, so they can spread the word and provide required reach for your messages.

2. Maven

Mavens are information experts. They accumulate incredible knowledge and are recognized, trusted experts in their field. Typically, they are early adapters of new technologies.

3. Salesmen

Salesmen are very charismatic persuaders. They have very strong negotiation skills and can make people buy into your idea.

Depending on what message you want to spread, you can make use of the different types of influencers. Important is to recognize and identify the few key influencers that will have the real impact.

The strength of weak ties.

Another interesting phenomena shows that loose social network connections, i.e. weak ties, can be a great source of differentiation and diversity.

1. Frequency
Strong ties are more likely to share the same or similar information. Contacts are more likely to consume and respond to information from stronger ties.

2. Grouping
Interacting with a group of contacts frequently, also raises the likelihood that these contacts will interact more frequently with each other. As a result, homogeneous groups of strong ties emerge.

3. Breath
On the other hand, the vast majority of information comes from contacts that we interact with less frequently, due to typically larger volume of weak ties in the network.

4. Novelty
Often, weak ties act as gatekeepers to disconnected groups and teams. As a result, they can enrich discussions with new perspectives and information, which might have left out by a group of strong ties.

«It's time to transform your business
for the new social reality.»

«Social media is changing how we connect and share in our personal lives and—increasingly—in business. Our customers are just as likely to look for us on Facebook as they are to visit our corporate website. Internally, we work more productively when we can easily collaborate with our colleagues online. Weaving a social context into your business is quickly becoming a prerequisite for success. It's time to transform your business for the new social reality. It's time to delight your customers by connecting to them— and to your employees—in new and powerful ways. Welcome to the Social Enterprise.»

Salesforce.com,
"The Social Enterprise",
January 2012.

Collaboration

Put simply, collaboration means working together towards common targets. Successful sales collaboration consists of 3 critical elements:

1. Teamwork
It is about people sharing information, exchanging documents and opinions. Sometimes organized in public groups, to get broad input on the next sales campaign. But very often in small teams, to collaborate on a specific sales opportunity in an intimate way.

2. Project Management
In fact, every sales opportunity is a small project requiring resource orchestration and task synchronization in order to make best use of the collective knowledge and relationships of its members.

3. Communication
Finally, we can make use of online communication tools like discussion forums, chat, video chat and web meetings to effectively communicate with each other.

Depending on the complexity of the opportunity, there is a direct correlation between sales effectiveness and collaboration.

Short: No sales without collaboration.

«Social Business Software is transforming business as we know it. And driving breakthroughs in productivity, sales, product innovation, and employee and customer satisfaction.»

«Traditional enterprise applications reinforce hierarchies and create siloes. With Social Business, information flows freely. Social Business Software lets people form self-organizing communities, discover each other and connect – instantly. Work gets done far more naturally and faster than ever before.»

Jive Software,
"New to Social Business?",
January 2012.

Enterprise 2.0

Described as Facebook for the enterprise, social business software helps users to collaborate more effectively, internally as well as externally. Typically, it consists of the following functionality.

1. Profiles
Users can manage their profile information including contact details, competencies, business background, education and current responsibilities. This is especially valuable to identify appropriate project resources.

2. Connections
Users can follow and connect with each other in order to stay up-to-date on collegues and their activities.

3. Real-Time Update
By following other users, groups, sales opportunities or even customers and competitors, users can receive a network stream of status updates in real-time.

4. Teamrooms
Every sales opportunity is a project. Users can join groups to share information, exchange documents and manage project tasks and calender.

5. Chat
Integrated presence management and chat functionality facilitates communication.

Shake up your B2B sales by leveraging the power of collaboration, social networks and CRM.

Social Sales means seeing relationships as assets and investing into the social capital of your company, your sales networks, in order to win strategic opportunities and grow your business. It provides a structured approach to relationship-driven decision-making. Over time, it has evolved into a comprehensive sales approach to "identify, analyze and act". But how does a SocialSalesMap look like? What is a SocialSalesIndex? And how can a SocialSalesMatrix help you in defining the most effective action plan?

V. Social Sales

«Social Sales represents a new way of fueling sales force productivity, eliminating functional silos and becoming more responsive to customer demands. »

«At Accenture, we believe any organization can benefit from a Social Sales capability. Our research and experience have shown that top sales forces across all industries achieve an optimal balance of data, technology, process and talent. In doing so, they master both the art and science of sales. Social sales provides a low-cost mechanism by which companies can not only achieve the balance of skills they need, but also bridge the art/science gap. This, in turn, helps organizations improve their sales force productivity across the sales lifecycle, from identifying prospects to winning the deal. »

Accenture,

"Social Sales - Collaborating for high performance",

2011.

Social Sales Opportunities

Sales has always been challenging. Especially strategic sales.

1. Relationship
Engaging multiple levels of decision-makers across complex value networks requires a very structured and analytic approach to relationship-driven decision-making.

2. Soft Factors
Effectively navigating politics by incorporating social factors will reduce the risk of failure and avoid unwanted surprises.

3. Collaboration
Collaborating effectively with internal stakeholders, channel partners and influencers can shorten the sales cycle, increase your win rate and help you grow your business.

4. Social Media
Making best use of social networks to identify and engage relevant influencers.

Identify, Analyze, Act

Social Sales is about mapping and analyzing Social Sales networks to define the most effective, relationship-driven sales strategy and action plan.

1. Identify
In a first step, we need to identify and map decision-makers, influencers, partners and customer contacts (and their relationships) into a social network graph. By visualizing the results, you can get a first idea of potential options.

2. Analyze
Based on the information available, who is the most important contact for us to work with? Where should we focus our resources? Which contacts to engage first?

Applying social network analysis (SNA) to complex B2B sales can provide answers to some of those questions.

3. Act
Sales teams want to win, so they need to focus their efforts on the most important tasks. By using the above visualization and analysis, they have the transparency and confidence in place, to build the most effective sales strategy and action plan leveraging their existing relationships networks. A sales network lives. Actions will turn into new identified contacts and changed relationships. Managing it in iterative circles will help you to get the most of your sales engagement.

1. Identify

Like in classical buying center analysis, it is important to understand the key players of a deal. The difference with using Social Sales methodologies is that we can also map the relationships between them in form of a network, so it helps to understand how the influence moves and where the social center of gravity is.

1. Decision-Maker
Who are the relevant authorities in the specific buying process, formally or informally?

2. Influencer
Who are the internal and external people with the most (potential) influence on the buying decision?

3. Partner
Are there any channel partners that we should bring to the table? Does the customer have a preference for specific distributors, integrators, design houses or consultancies?

4. Internal Support
Do we need an executive sponsorship? Who in the account team has relevant relationships to leverage? How can we get support from the right people in the product or service team?

Shot: SocialSalesMap

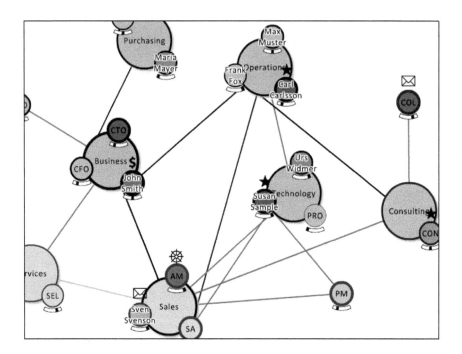

A picture tells more than words. And faster. When it comes to networks, traditional tables and forms reach their limits. Instead, maps can help you telling the story.

SocialSalesMap

A SocialSalesMap is a graphical representation of a sales network. It helps to identify, engage and manage key influencers and decision-makers effectively.

1. Simple information access
It carries information on companies, teams, contacts, relationships and actions.

2. Graphical visualization
It displays key data like influence, position, names, functions, actions, roles and relationships directly on the map.

3. Collaboration
It enables multi-user access, simulations, action and milestone management to facilitate teamwork and effective collaboration.

4. Social Network Analysis (SNA)
SNA allows you to segment your contacts and aggregate drivers into an interactive graph to ease sales life and support pro-active decision-making.

5. Smart Integration
By integrating to Outlook, LinkedIn, Xing, Facebook, Twitter and Skype as well as leading CRM systems, you can re-use existing contact and relationship information.

Social Relationships

A relationship lives. It can grow or dry out over time. In order to analyze networks, we need to capture and understand the relationships in more detail, especially...

1. Relationship Intensity
The frequency of interactions and touchpoints drives the intensity of a relationship.

2. Relationship Quality
Working with someone on a daily base makes up a high intensity, but it doesn't mean you have a very intimate relationship. Instead, the relationship quality is defined by the mutual acceptance, intimacy and trust. It can be both, positive or negative.

3. Relationship Type
The nature and kind of relationship can be very different reaching from kinship to friendship, from membership to business.

4. Direction
Some relationships like member (of) or reporting (to) will also feature a clear direction.

Regarding sales, it is important to understand the different parameters in order to judge the potential cross-influence between the counterparts.

2. Analyze

Based on the information available, who is the most important contact for us to work with? Where should we focus our resources? Which contacts to engage first?

Applying social network analysis (SNA) to complex B2B sales can provide effective answers to some of those questions. Assuming, a first estimate of the influence of a contact is available, we can use SNA algorithms to calculate the overall importance of any contact within a sales network, i.e. the so-called SocialSalesIndex (SSI).

1. Individual and team Influence
The more influence my team has, the higher my importance for the specific opportunity. Specific roles are also strong drivers of influence.

2. Relationships
The underlying logic is simple. The more relationships someone has to other important stakeholders, the higher her indirect influence. The more intense those relationships, the better.

The SocialSalesIndex (SSI) is an indicator of social influence of teams and/or persons in a sales network based on network topology as well as relevance and intensity of her relationships (calculated as Eigenvector Centrality).

It can be used for ranking key decision makers in terms of importance. The higher the SocialSalesIndex, the more important the contact for the sales decision.

Shot: SocialSalesMatrix

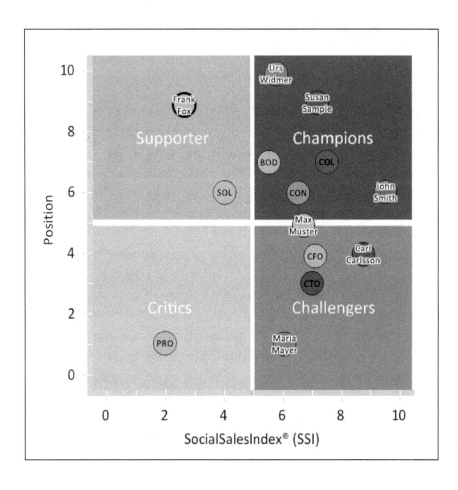

Engineers like matrix diagrams. But business people love it. Looking at the SocialSalesMatrix, we can focus our sales efforts on the most important targets and hopefully avoid talking to the wrong audience.

SocialSalesMatrix

In a SocialSalesMatrix, all contacts are being segmented by importance (SocialSalesIndex) as well as their pro/contra position. As a result, we receive manageable, actionable groups.

1. Challengers
It's very important to understand the most important, but critical decision-makers to decide about potential mitigation. A hunter will focus most of her efforts here.

2. Critics
In the mid-term, a farmer will try to improve the position of less important contacts through better sales, marketing and service engagement with reasonable effort.

3. Supporter
This group can be used very well for a positive "Grundrauschen", even if their immediate importance is limited.

4. Champions
These are our most important promoters. If we manage to turn all decision-makers into champions, we will win.

Shot: Driver Analysis

A spider graph helps to understand and focus on the mission-critical drivers of your sales opportunity. Tip: You might also map the capabilities of your partners to the spider, so you can complement your skills.

Driver Analysis

Once we have understood the sales network and its players, we can now think about which are the key decision criteria that we need to work on to secure the deal.

1. Driver Assessment

Decision criteria can vary a lot by target group and buying phase. The business team might want to facilitate profitable growth, purchasing wants to reduce costs and the technology team might look for new innovation, compatibility or reliability. In a first step, we need to identify those key drivers and assess their importance on a fixed scale.

2. Consolidation

When consolidating the different needs into a common view, we can re-use the results of the SNA. The driver of teams with the highest influence on the buying decision will have more weight.

3. Gap Analysis

In order to do a gap analysis, we can now match our capabilities against the consolidated, weighted needs. What's the perceived contribution in terms of growth, price and innovation? How do we rank compared to competition?

Shot: Act

You need both: An effective sales strategy and a professional execution. The best plan is obsolete if you don't have the tools and structure in place to follow-up.

3. Act

Every sales network is different, so is the sales strategy and action plan. Important is to follow an analytic, structured approach, understand the strategic options and apply them most effectively.

1. Targeting
If relationships to key influencers or decision-makers exist, we can target and engage them directly. The good thing with targeting is that we have full control of our message and can actively handle objections.

2. Bridging
In case no direct relationships exist yet, we can establish bridges by either being introduced to the target or for future channeling.

3. Channeling
Sometimes, it can be most effective to use bridges respectively indirect relationships to channel our message instead of trying to build up a direct relationship. This is especially true if close contacts of the target audience act as trusted advisor.

4. Bypassing
In order to minimize dependency on existing bridges or gatekeepers, we might want to neutralize them by establishing direct relationships or building up alternative paths.

In reality, the most effective sales strategy will always incorporate a mix of different Social Sales actions.

«In today's workplace, people have emerged as the most
valuable asset to unlocking the power
of information and ideas.»

«To innovate and remain competitive, organizations need to provide the
right tools, culture, and IT ecosystem for employees, business partners,
suppliers, and customers to communicate and collaborate.»

IDC,
"Enterprise Collaboration and Social Solutions.",
2012.

Collaboration

Sometimes, orchestrating the internal team can be more challenging than working with the customer.

1. Leadership
The opportunity owner is responsible to coordinate the overall effort. She needs to build the team, assign roles and responsibilities, as well as coach and support the team members. By visualizing your own team on your sales network you will increase transparency and commitment.

2. Weekly Opportunity Reviews
Regular status meetings, either as online conferences or in person are a prerequisite to keep everybody aligned and engaged.

3. Notifications
Real-time information on contacts, customers and partners will keep your team up-to-date on the latest status and actions and help you to re-act fast, if needed.

4. Win/Loss Analysis
There's a lot you can learn from a good debriefing. Review the key milestones and how your sales network has evolved over time. What would you do differently today and what would you re-do the same way again?

«Nothing is easier than loosing a competitive edge in the marketplace. You just have to stand still.»

Marcel Dobler, CEO, Digitec

The Road to Success.

Social Sales will not happen overnight, but can be developed in stages.

1. Internal Collaboration
Break the silos. Build diverse, multi-functional, cross-group teams to manage specific opportunities. Run brainstorming workshops to leverage your social capital most effectively.

2. External Collaboration
Enhance your sales network by making your partners become part of your team. Engage influencers strategically. Ask your customer supporters and champions to help you on your journey.

3. Standardization
Align your tools, processes and terminology into a common Social Sales framework. Define local superusers to provide interactive trainings and gather continuous feedback.

4. Advanced Deployment
SocialSalesMaps have entered the boardroom and are a core element of your account planning. Pipeline reviews have turned into "social" opportunity reviews. Sales incentives are aligned with social objectives.

5. Strategic Engagement
Enhancing your social capital is the core driving force of your growth strategy. Social Sales has become part of your corporate culture and DNA.

«The implications for a salesperson are simple. They have to understand that generating leads, managing opportunities and closing deals need fresh approaches and skills in utilizing tools that help enrich customer insights.»

«Because whether it's a B2B or B2C sale, the customer is expecting you, the sales maven and your company, to know them and what they want. That means that sales intelligence and engaging in the networks the customer participates in are of critical importance.»

Oracle/The Customer Collective,
"The Art of Social Sales",
2009.

Summary

It will be hard to ignore the changes and opportunities provided by collaboration, social networks and CRM.

Sales is about People. And Social Sales is about engaging the right people at the right time in order to win. It provides a fresh approach to master the complexities of B2B sales by making the best use of the social capital of your company.

In brief, Social Sales addresses the need to
1. Identify and map influencers and decision-makers
2. Analyze, manage and enhance sales networks
3. Effectively act on relationship-driven sales strategies

And finally to collaborate effectively across the sales cycle, internally as well as externally.

If you believe, that people and relationships are the driving forces of sales success in your business, Social Sales is designed for you.

What are you waiting for?

Social Sales. The Book.

This page is intentionally left blank.

V. Social Sales.

This page is intentionally left blank.

Abbreviations

AIDA – Attention, Interest, Desire, Action

BANT – Budget, Authority, Need, Timeline

CRM – Customer Relationship Management

COS – Cost of Sales

NPS – Net Promoter Score

ROI – Return of Investment

RFQ – Request for Quotation

RFP – Request for Proposal

SKU - Stock Keeping Unit

SME – Subject Matter Expert

SMM – Social Media Monitoring

SNA – Social Network Analysis

SRM – Supplier Relationship Management

SSI – SocialSalesIndex

POEM – Paid, Owned, Earned Media

ZMOT – Zero Moment of Truth

Recommended Readings

Accenture, "Social Sales - Collaborating for high performance",2011.

CSO Insights,"Revenue 2012: Making it Happen Versus Hoping it Happens", January 2012.

Gartner Group, "Magic Quadrant for Social CRM", July 2011.

IBM Corporation, "The Social Business - Advent of a new age", February 2011.

Luc Galoppin,"Social Architecture, a Manifesto", January 2011.

McKinsey & Company, "The rise of the networked enterprise: Web 2.0 finds its payday.", April 2011.

Oracle/The Customer Collective, "The Art of Social Sales", 2009.

Checklist

1. Discovery

[ ] Do we have an <Opportunity Owner> assigned?

[ ] Does the <Opportunity Owner> confirm her/his role?

[ ] Do we have a first idea of the customer budget?

[ ] Do we have a first relationship to the customer?

2. Qualification

[ ] Is the <Budget Owner> identified?

[ ] Does the <Budget Owner> confirm the budget?

[ ] Is the <Ultimate Authority> identified?

[ ] Do we have a first idea of the customer drivers?

[ ] Do we know the timeline?

[ ] Did the customer confirm the timeline?

3. Pre-Proposal

[ ] Did we receive a request for information?

[ ] Is the <Proposal Lead> identified?

[ ] Does the <Proposal Lead> confirm her/his role?

[ ] Do we have a direct relationship to the <Ultimate Authority>?

[ ] Do we have a relationship to the majority of important players?

[ ] Did we identify potential partners?

[ ] Did we establish relationships to the potential partners?

[ ] Did we validate the drivers of the customer?

[ ] Did the important players confirm their key drivers?

[ ] Are our capabilities close to the drivers of the customer?

[ ] Has the timeline being updated/reconfirmed?

[ ] Did we provide a draft budget proposal to the customer?

4. Proposal

[ ] Did we receive a request for proposal?

[ ] Is the <Contract Signatory> identified?

[ ] Can we turn the <Ultimate Authority> into a <Champion>?

[ ] Did we turn the majority of <Critics> into <Supporters>?

[ ] Did we turn the majority of <Challengers> into <Champions>?

[ ] Do we have the support of potential partners?

[ ] Did the partner(s) confirm their support and championship?

[ ]Did we re-validate the drivers of the customer?

[ ] Did the important players confirm the key drivers?

[ ] Do our capabilities match ALL customer drivers?

[ ] Has the timeline been updated/reconfirmed?

[ ] Did we provide a final proposal to the customer?

5. Negotiation

[ ] Did we receive a verbal commitment?

[ ] Did we establish relationship to the <Contract Signatory>?

[ ] Do we have the support of the <Contract Signatory>?

6. Award

[ ] Did the customer award the contract?

[ ] Did we win?

Social Sales. The Book.

This page is intentionally left blank.

About the Author

Andreas Uthmann is a consultant and business developer with a strong passion for technology and innovation.

He is the founder and CEO of Blueconomics Business Solutions GmbH (www.blueconomics.com) supporting customers to drive B2B sales, marketing and service effectiveness by leveraging the power of collaboration, social networks and CRM.

He was born in Westphalia/Germany and lives in Zürich/Switzerland.

This page is intentionally left blank.

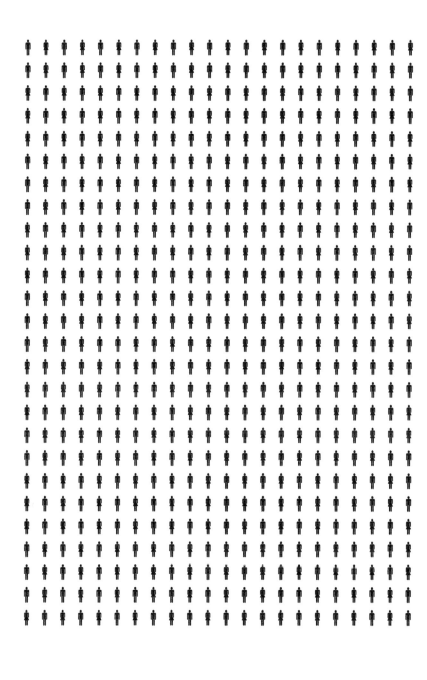

This page is intentionally left blank.

This page is intentionally left blank.

This page is intentionally left blank.

This page is intentionally left blank.

This page is intentionally left blank.